D1740887

PREPARE YOURSELF FOR A WONDERFUL LIFE-CHANGING EXPERIENCE

PREPARE YOURSELF FOR A WONDERFUL LIFE-CHANGING EXPERIENCE

Richard Franza

Rev. date: 12/28/2018

To order additional copies of this book, contact:
Xlibris
1-888-795-4274
www.Xlibris.com
Orders@Xlibris.com
789882

CONTENTS

My special message to you:

Prepare yourself for a wonderful life-changing experience.

Richard R. Franza

'A golden opportunity of having a wonderful life-changing experience has come your way. Seize this excellant opportunity now because this may very well be a once in a lifetime chance for you.'

Richard R. Franza

This Book Is Of Immense Value

On our journey through this life

We can choose this or that,

Let's be wise with our choices,

Let's choose a life of peace,

Let's choose a life of happiness,

Let's choose a life of harmony,

And not a life of problems and strife.

Now is your chance

In this eternal dance

To enhance

Your life upon this earth,

Take advantage of this chance

As another day has been given birth.

This book will guide you well in life,

Take advantage of this advantage now,

Get the most out of what is in this book,

I want you to have

The best life that you can possibly have.

Go now and read on,

See for yourself that

This book is of immense value.

Richard R. Franza

This book is dedicated to my two wonderful sons, David and Daniel, and my five wonderful grandchildren, Anne, TJ, Selena, Leah, and Alice. May this book serve my two wonderful sons well, and may this book also serve my five wonderful grandchildren well when they are of proper age to read it. A special dedication goes to my wonderful parents, Rocco and Judy, whom had departed from this earth for good. May they be resting peacefully wherever they may be.

Introduction

I T GIVES ME great pleasure to have this opportunity to share this book with you. I want you to know that I am very fond of this book. This book may very well be one of the most important books that you will ever read. I can state this claim with absolute certainty because there is an immense amount of vital information in this book. You should easily be able to detect this if you were to read this book in it's entirety. I had went out of my way in order to provide the readers of this book with insight into many important issues in life.

I am an Operation Desert Storm veteran whom deeply loves America. I am very proud to be an American, but I must admit to you right now that I am not proud of what America had became in these modern times. I had included a topic in this book about the glorious Golden Age of America because I want other Americans in particular to know that us Americans are depriving ourselves of having such a magnificent life in America because we are settling for what America had became. Us Americans must strive to bring out the best in ourselves so that we can bring out the best in America.

I also consider myself as an amateur environmentalist. I had included a topic in this book about the fact that us humans have a tragic fate ahead of us because we are slowly destroying our natural world and consuming precious resources at such an alarming rate. Us humans must now take strong measures towards further protecting and preserving our natural world because we are ignorantly creating a hellish world for our own future generations to live in. We also must conserve precious resources and also look to further utilize natural means such as solar power in order to satisfy our strong thirst for energy sources.

I also consider myself as an amateur philosopher. I had included a topic in this book that is about the need for us humans to be philosophers in life. We must change our ways and 'put on our thinking caps' in order to not only bring meaning to life, but also so that we can greatly help to improve the condition of this seemingly hopeless world.

I am also a spiritualist whom has been practicing certain techniques for about seven years now that had greatly helped me to have a wonderful life-changing experience. I had included certain topics in this book about spiritual matters and the techniques that

I am currently practicing. I truly hope that I will do a great job in encouraging you to practice the techniques that are in this book so that you will have an excellant opportunity to have a wonderful life-changing experience as I had. By practicing the techniques that are in this book, you should develop yourself spiritually and have a much better life as what had happened to me.

Since my main goal is to encourage you to practice the techniques that are in this book, I think that it is only fair that I share with you right now the reason why I had motivated myself to discover and begin to practice the techniques that are in this book.

You see, it all started about seven years ago when I was a crack cocaine addict, miserable much of the time, very much so materialistic, an unknower of my true natural self in which gave me no chance of being my true natural self, and I was also suffering from a mental illness. I was totally disgusted with myself and with life about seven years ago as I was in dire need of change. It was about seven years ago that I had made a conscious decision to do what it takes to change for the better. It was about seven years ago that I had come to realize that the first thing that I had needed to do was to control my mind before I can do anything else with effectiveness. This is when I had discovered and began to practice the first and most important technique of being in a constant meditative state which is about controlling our minds. As time progressed I had discovered other techniques and began to practice them. Within a relatively short period of time I had not only quit smoking crack cocaine, but also I had became desireless towards abusing alcohol and all illegal drugs, I was much more happier, I became spiritual, I had discovered my true natural self as I was my true natural self on certain occasions, and my mental illness had became greatly alleviated. It was because of practicing these techniques that I had completely transformed my life for the much better. This is most definetly a story of success. If this could happen to me, this could happen to anyone else. I am no exception to the rule. If your life is not going well for you, I want you to know that you now have an excellant opportunity to make your life much better, but first of all you must be willing to do what it takes to make your life much better. I strongly suggest to you to practice the techniques that are in this book.

There are other topics in this book that may also be of interest to you. I had went out of my way in order to provide you with an immense amount of vital information in this book that should greatly serve you towards having a wonderful life-changing experience. Don't pass this golden opportunity to have a wonderful life-changing experience on by. You deserve all the best that this life can afford to you.

At this moment in time you may be wondering to yourself if whether or not I am a creditable source for information. All that I can tell you right now is that I am a very creditable source for information because of my own personal experiences in life. Life had taught me well. I am sharing with you aspects in life that are working well for me. I want you to have the kind of life that I am now having as it seems to be that my life is getting better and better with each passing day because of practicing the techniques that are in this book.

I know very well that you may be thinking to yourself right now that it is very overwhelming to practice fifteen techniques. Think again. It is not overwhelming to practice the fifteen techniques that are in this book unless you have very little spare time to practice them. I feel that it is essential to practice the first two techniques that are in this book, then choose which one's out of the other thirteen techniques to practice.

You are the boss if you were to practice the techniques that are in this book. I will only offer you suggestions about how I currently practice these techniques. You can practice them any which way you choose to practice them. If you were to practice the techniques that are in this book, you must also have plenty of patience and perseverance especially in the beginning because it may take quite some time for you to properly practice them, and it may take quite some time for the techniques to take effect.

I am not in the conversion business. Come as you are. You can be a member of any religion, you can follow any philosophy in life, it doesn't matter because by practicing the techniques that are in this book, this should serve you well towards enhancing your life experiences.

As a reminder, there are no guarantees that you will have a wonderful life-changing experience if you were to practice the techniques that are in this book, and I am not responsible for your outcome if you were to practice them, but I firmly believe that if you were to properly practice the techniques that are in this book, you should eventually one day have a wonderful life-changing experience.

That's all that I wish to share with you in this introduction. I will now let you read onto the first topic in this book, but before I do, I would like to tell you that may you not only enjoy reading this book, but also may this book serve you well.

Oh yeah, before I forget to mention this to you, I had also included a special bonus in this book in which is an outline of one hundred suggestions that should greatly help you towards having a truly wonderful life-changing experience. I had also included in this book some philosophical quotes of the day, certain facts about me, a closing poem, and a closing topic. It is now time to read the first topic in this book: 'The Veil Of An Illusion.' Prepare yourself for an exciting adventure as you traverse through the pages of this book.

The Veil Of An Illusion

I T IS A few minutes before one o'clock in the morning right now and here I am starting to write about the very first topic that is in this book. I am still a little tired after waking up from a descent nap. Let's see how well I will do with writing about this topic. Let's see how I am going to start to write it.

Okay, I am going to start to write about this topic with something to make you think about for a while. What do you think that the physical universe that we exist in is truly is? Do you think that the physical universe is an unfolding dream? Do you think that the physical universe is a fantasy? Do you think that the physical universe is a mirage? Do you think that the physical universe is an illusion? Or, do you think that the physical universe is real? I will now give you some time to think about this... What do you think about the physical universe that we exist in? Please pause for a few moments in order to think about this.

I kind of suspect that I know what you think about the physical universe that we exist in. You probably think that the physical universe that we exist in is real, right? Right! Well, if this is the case, you may be in for a big surprise to find out that the physical universe that we exist in is not real in it's truest sense, but it is an illusion. Say what? That's right. The physical universe that we exist in is not real in it's truest sense, but it is an illusion. You may be wondering to yourself about this right now. I mean, what gives me the right to say this to you right now?

You see, according to spirituality, anything that was created, undergoes changes, and eventually perishes is not real in it's truest sense. It is in fact an illusion. If it is true that what many scientists claim that the physical universe that we exist in was created, we all do know that it undergoes changes, and it will eventually perish one day, then we can clearly see that the physical universe that we exist in is not real in it's truest sense, but it is an illusion. I know that what I had just told you may not make any sense at all because the physical universe that we exist in seems so real. No one can deny this.

If what I had just told you is the truth, then it is safe for me to say that everything in this physical world is not real in it's truest sense, but it is all an illusion. Us humans are being delusional into thinking and believing that this physical world and everything in it is so real.

We are most definetly being deceived. I am well aware of the fact that what I am suggesting to you right now may also not make any sense to you because us humans are conditioned to think and believe that this physical world and everything in it is so real. You can easily detect that we think and believe in this manner just by observing how others converse with each other. Quite often you should hear them make such a big fuss over matters that deals with this physical world, dramatizing them at times. Not even our own physical bodies are real. Say what? That's right. Not even our own physical bodies are real. This is the reason why it would be to our best interest to not to identify ourselves with our physical bodies. Instead we should identify ourselves with the part of our being that is real. We should identify ourselves with whom we truly are, indestructable, eternal spirits. And, if it is true that our physical bodies are not real in it's truest sense, then there is no reason why we should fear death. Death in reality does not exist. There is only life. Most likely we go through a process of rebirth, this thing that we call being reincarnated. We may exist in a different physical form for eternity. Who knows for sure.

Just imagine what life would be like for us humans upon this earth if we were to come to a full understanding that this physical world and everything in it is just an illusion. Chances are we wouldn't have a deep love affair with money, we wouldn't be so greedy, selfish, possessive, impressionists. I am quite certain that life upon this earth for us humans would be much better for us all if we were to live the truth.

It is quite obvious to me that there is a veil that is casted right before our eyes that disguises the fact that this world and everything in it is not real, but in fact an illusion. In order to pierce through this veil and see the truth of it all, we should develop ourselves spiritually by practicing the techniques that are in this book. I had developed myself spiritually over the last seven years because of practicing these techniques. I now have a much better understanding of our place in this physical universe. I now know that it ain't worth getting carried away by anything that occurs in this world because I know that this world and everything in it is not truly real in it's truest sense.

If you are entangled in matters that pertain to this world and you are not able to pierce through the veil that is disguising an illusion, I strongly suggest to you to practice the techniques that are in this book and eventually one day you should be able to pierce through this veil of an illusion as I had done.

Oh yeah, before I end this topic, I must tell you that even though this physical world and everything that is in it, including our physical bodies, is just an illusion, we should still strive to make our temporal stay here upon this earth as pleasant as we can possibly make it, and we should also try to make our world a much better place to live in in order for our own future generations to come to benefit. It doesn't make any sense to me that us humans are creating so many problems for ourselves and are also in fact slowly creating a hellish world for our own future generations to come to live in. This world of ours is sadly a hopeless world mainly because of the actions of the leaders of this world, and our lack of care and concern. The truth of the matter is that the leaders of this world are slowly guiding us to our own inevitable destruction, and here we are, foolishly following the dictates of the leaders of the world. When is there going to ever be leaders of the world whom are working towards truly benefitting mankind and our own future generations to come? And, when are us humans going to wake up and realize that we are traveling on a road that is leading us to destruction?

Time is running out for us humans. If we continue to conduct our lives in the same manner in which we are currently conducting them eventually one day the human race will become extinct. This may take quite some, but it is bound to happen. It is now time for us humans to wake up and put an end to caring about penny-ante things like if our favorite sporting team wins a game or not, and care about important things that could improve the current condition for us humans in this world. It is foolish to only care about making money, having fun, entertaining ourselves, partying, driving fancy cars, and so on when at the same time we couldn't care less about important issues that are very much so problematic that will seemingly never be resolved mainly because the leaders of the world are basically ignoring these important issues.

The truth of the matter is that not only us humans are creating a great deal of problems for ourselves, but also we had created a very dangerous world for us to live in. You can blame much of this on the leaders of the world and us common people whom are following the dictates of the leaders of the world. It is a severe case of the blind leading the blind. Boy oh boy, what kind of dismal world that I was born into!

Our True Purpose In Life

ALL OF THIS negativity that I had written about in the last topic. I am a little ashamed of myself because here I am, 'Mr. Positive' to others, a man whom brags about being positive and not focusing on anything negative, and I had just written about some negative things. Hey, I am only human. I guess that it's okay to be negative at times if it is necessary to do so.

Anyway, for most of my life I had never taken the time to try to understand if us humans have a true purpose in life or not, and if we do, then what is it. For most of my life I had other things on my mind to deal with, therefore it had never dawned on me if us humans have a true purpose in life or not, and if we do, then what is it. This had all changed about seven years ago when I had started to practice the first technique that is in this book. I had developed an interest in trying to find out if us humans have a true purpose in life or not, and if we do, then what is it.

I come to believe that there are many purposes in life that we can have such as worshipping God, being a success in life, serving others, procreating, and so on. I come to believe that these things are just purposes in life. I am not interested in just purposes in life. I would like to know with absolute certainty if us humans have a true purpose in life or not, and if we do, then what is our true purpose in life. I guess that I will never know with absolute certainty about these things, but I can make a good assumption about them.

You see, it makes good sense to me that us humans do have a true purpose in life, that we were not taken out of our own heavenly home and sent to earth for no apparent reason. There has to be a good reason for us humans to be existing upon this earth I come to believe. If this is the case, then what is the reason why us humans exist upon this earth, what is our true purpose in life?

After practicing some of the techniques that are in this book for quite some time, I had came to realize that our true purpose in life is to discover and become our true natural selves so that we can have an opportunity to create a replica upon this earth of our true heavenly home. In other words, our true purpose in life is to transform ourselves from our lowly animal nature and into our true spiritual selves so that we can express all of the finer qualities that our true spiritual selves possesses, and be able to transform our earthly existence into a heavenly paradise. What is your opinion in this matter? Do you agree with me on this or not?

If I am correct about us humans having a true purpose in life and what this true purpose in life is, then it is safe for me to say to you right now that many of us humans are missing the point of our existence upon this earth. Many of us humans are wasting their lives away by chasing after 'rainbows in the sky.' When are us humans ever going to wake up and put an end to chasing after money, great sex, entertainment, having fun, fancy cars, and so on, and live our lives according to the dictates of whom we truly are because in essence, we are spiritual beings whom are having a humanly experience.

All that I have left to tell you in this topic is that if you were to practice the techniques that are in this book, eventually one day you should have a similar understanding as I do about us humans having a true purpose in life and what this true purpose in life is. Find out for yourself if what I had told you in this topic makes good sense or not.

A Light In The World

ACCORDING TO MY current understanding, Jesus Christ was considered to have been the light of the world as is stated in the Holy Bible. I come to believe that this statement should be taken literally because Jesus Christ was truly a light in the world, and this statement should be taken nonliterally because he also had dispelled the darkness of ignorance. Talking about ignorance, it seems to be that there is so much ignorance in the world (There I go again, being negative). This ignorance mainly stems from us humans being conditioned to be a certain way. This is one of the reasons why we should discover and become our true natural selves by practicing the techniques that are in this book.

Anyway, I come to believe that each and everyone of us humans have the potential to be a light in the world. We can do this if we knew how to do it. If you were to think in scientific terms that our physical bodies are composed of atoms that I come to believe vibrate at a certain frequency, I think that the atoms that composes our bodies can be raised to a higher frequency in which could be very useful in the healing of ourselves and raise us to a higher level.

Everything is energy in one form or another. Everything is vibrations. If you were to understand these two principles, then you are most definetly traveling on the right road in life. Even the most solid objects are composed of atoms that vibrate at a certain frequency. I know that this may not make any sense, but what makes sense in life anyway?

The human mind is a very powerful tool to possess. I know that you had heard of that cliche: 'Mind over matter.' Us humans have the potential to do extraordinary things with the proper use of our minds. I come to believe also that certain scientists claim that we use only about ten percent of our brains. If this is the truth, can you imagine what we will be capable of doing if we were to use one hundred percent of our brains.

On a personal note, I come to believe that I am a light in the world at times. I come to believe this because at times I am experiencing a certain glow that emanates from my body. There were even times that others had made certain comments about this. It's hard to describe it in words, but you should know darn well if you are being a light in the world. It's as if your soul is shining through.

At this moment in time you may be wondering why I had included this topic in this book that is suppose to be about a wonderful life-changing experience. I can't blame you for this. The reason why I had included this topic in this book is that by becoming a light in the world, we did in fact have a wonderful life-changing experience. We had taken our bodies that was just a lump of mass and transformed them into a light that shines brightly for all others to see.

If you would like to become a light in the world if you are not one already, I strongly suggest to you to practice the techniques that are in this book. Go now and try to brightly shine like the sun for all eyes to see.

Entering Into The Stream

A CCORDING TO MY current understanding, it is in Buddhism in which you will find the teaching of entering into the stream. You are not to take this literally of course and enter into an actual stream; this would be very foolish if you were to take this literally and actually enter into a stream.

You may be wondering to yourself right now about what is meant to enter into the stream. I can't blame you for this, but I want you to know that it is not easy to explain to anyone about what is meant to enter into the stream. Here I go again, trying to explain something to you that you must experience for yourself because words can't explain it very well.

It was just a few hours ago when I had entered into the stream for several minutes. It was such a wonderful experience for me as it happened naturally. The best way that I can describe the experience is that I had felt a total emptiness of thoughts and emotions as I was experiencing energy flowing through my body and emanating outward into space directly above my head. I was overjoyed by the experience and I wish that I will experience it more often as time progresses.

Look, I come to believe that I had entered into the stream on certain occasions. Life had slowed down for me and I was in a state of pure ecstacy when this had happened to me. In total honesty, I really don't have anything more to tell you about this except that it is because I take the time to practice the techniques that are in this book that I am able to enter into the stream on certain occasions. It truly is such a wonderful experience when I enter into the stream. Oh yeah, I had forgotten to mention something else to you about entering into the stream. You see, when I enter into the stream, it feels as if I am going with the flow, allowing the energy to flow nice and smoothly as I am very calm and peaceful. I come to believe that I am truly being my true natural self when I enter into the stream. What better way is there to have a wonderful life-changing experience than to develop yourself spiritually to a point in which you can enter into the stream at will?

Synchronizing With The Celestial Bodies

HERE WE ARE, us humans living in a life that is full of mystery. Ain't it a darn shame that modern man is so entangled in this artificial life that we have created. We had lost our sense of living the mystery because of this. Everything in this life is a marvel to behold, but here we are, many of us humans living in today's modern world, taking everything for granted. I guess that this was bound to happen. Us humans basically have everything laid out for ourselves. All that we need to do these days is to turn on a power switch of any electronic or electrical device and like magic these devices do what we want them to do. It wasn't like that many years ago before the advent of all of this modern technology and conveniences. Modern man had become too spoiled for sure.

There is a dear price to pay by living in this modern age with all of this technology and conveniences. Much of modern man had removed themselves from nature in order to dwell in concrete jungles. The ironic part of it all is that modern man should be much more happier than their ancestors whom had came before all of this technology and conveniences, but they are not. As a matter of fact, it seems to be that modern man is much less happier than their ancestors whom had come before all of this technology and conveniences. Life for modern man is full of problems and stress.

Another thing that happened to modern man is that they had lost a sense of their place in the universe. I come to believe that the ancestors from the distant past were much more 'tuned into' the celestial bodies. They had probably deeply understood that the celestial bodies had exerted a certain amount of influence upon them. The ancestors from the distant past had probably tried to be in harmony with the celestial bodies, trying to synchronize with them.

We all do know that the moon exerts an influence on us and on earth itself. If the moon can do these things as little of a celestial body as it is, then imagine how much more bigger celestial bodies exert an influence on us and earth itself.

The reason why I had included this topic in this book is that if we want to have a wonderful life-changing experience, we should put an end to living our lives artificially and try to synchronize ourselves with the celestial bodies. We should develop our psychic abilities first and become sensitive to the impressions that we receive from the celestial bodies. We should live a natural life by discovering and becoming our true natural selves. If you would like to discover and become your true natural self if you haven't done this already, I strongly suggest to you to practice the techniques that are in this book. Maybe I should now go to see an astrologer in order to determine what the future has in store for me. The only problem is that I know that even though the stars exerts an influence upon us humans from one extent to another extent, I am unsure if the alignment of the stars can tell us what we can expect in the future. Maybe I should save my money and use it to buy a good dinner and entertainment instead.

A Wonderful Life-Changing Experience

H OW DO YOU feel about what I had written in this book thus far? Do you think that I had done a good job with writing this book thus far? Are you able to clearly understand me with what I had written in this book thus far? Well, the good thing is that I believe that I had made this book clearly understandable thus far because I had hardly ever used terms that would most likely require the use of a dictionary in order to get the full understanding of what I am trying to tell you. I dislike reading something that is very complex to understand. Many writers write in such a way as to defeat their purpose of trying to get their message across to others. I try to avoid this for sure.

Anyway, at this moment in time you may be wondering to yourself just what I mean by a wonderful life-changing experience. Before I go into explaining this to you, I want to tell you about something that is very troubling. Why are many of us humans not approaching life properly? I mean, why on earth are many of us humans living their lives haphazourdly? The reason why I am raising this issue with you is that I currently live in a somewhat troubled neighborhood in East Flatbush, Brooklyn, New York. At times I experience confrontations with others in my neighborhood whom have nothing better to do than to start trouble with others for no reason. These individuals seek to prey on others whom they consider to be weak. This doesn't make any sense to me because by living their lives like that, they will never experience true happiness in their lives. How can anyone be truly happy in life if they are trying to spread misery around unto others? I had personally discovered by uplifting others, I experience much more happiness in my life. It is by spreading joy and good cheer in life, this makes me feel much better. By spreading misery unto others, this only brings us down. I truly wish that us humans can live very peacefully amongst each other so that we all can have a much better life together.

Anyway, what I mean by a wonderful life-changing experience is that there will be a major transformation in our lives that will make our lives well worth living. We will have developed ourselves spiritually and have a much better life. We will most definetly benefit in so many ways.

On a personal note, I had a wonderful life-changing experience in which my life was completely transformed into being what I want it to be for the most part. Don't get me wrong, I still go through life's ups and downs, but these ups and downs are most definetly occurring less frequently now. It seems to be that my life is getting better and better with each passing day. All the wonderful things that are happening to me is due to practicing the techniques that are in this book. I am very grateful and thankful to have discovered the techniques that are in this book, and to have the time and motivation to practice them. I am truly blessed to be in a position in life in which there is no need for me to work a regular job that leaves me with plenty of free time to practice the techniques that are in this book, but if I had to work a full-time job, I would probably still be practicing the techniques that are in this book by putting in much less time to practice them.

If you would like to have a wonderful life-changing experience in which you will experience a major transformation in your life that pertains to developing yourself spiritually and have a much better life, I strongly suggest to you to practice the techniques that are in this book. You have nothing to lose by practicing them, and alot to lose by not practicing them. If I can have a wonderful life-changing experience because of practicing the techniques that are in this book, so can anyone else. I am no exception to the rule. If your life is not going as well as you want it to be going, practice the techniques that are in this book, practice the techniques that are in this book, practice the techniques that are in this book!!! This is my battlecry to you. Start to practice the techniques that are in this book if you want to truly live the kind of life that you can only dream of living now. If you were to practice the techniques that are in this book, eventually one day you will be forever grateful to me for sharing these techniques with you. Just remember me during Christmas time (Just joking with you about this).

A Spiritual Lifestyle

TELL ME RIGHT now, what kind of a lifestyle that you are currently living? Is it a materialistic lifestyle or a spiritual lifestyle? Please pause for a few moments in order to think this over.

Are you finished with thinking this over for a few moments? Good! Let's now talk this over between us two. So, tell me, what is the answer to these questions? If the answer is a materialistic lifestyle, then you should pay very close attention to what I need to say to you in this topic. If the answer is a spiritual lifestyle, then you will probably already know what I need to say to you in this topic.

What can I say about a materialistic lifestyle, oh yeah, we had given a materialistic lifestyle a good try for a long time. Look at the kind of life that we are now living because of this, a life of emptiness for sure. We will never live a life of total satisfaction and complete happiness by living a materialistic lifestyle as we will always be in want of more. And, if we are living a materialistic lifestyle, we are prone to be money-hungered, selfish, greedy, possessive, impressionists. Living a materialistic lifestyle is not the proper approach to life, right? Right! You can blame much of the violence in our world on the fact that materialism is very prominent for us humans in the world that we live in. When are us humans going to evolve to a point in which we don't aggressively fight against each other and even kill each other as the animals do in the wild? There has got to be a much better way of living our lives.

A spiritual lifestyle is a far more superior way of living than a materialistic lifestyle for sure because of certain reasons such as if we were to live a spiritual lifestyle as opposed to a materialistic lifestyle, we would be living a much more of a natural life.

When I talk about a spiritual lifestyle, by no means am I talking about a religious lifestyle. I'm not the kind of man whom goes around telling others to praise the Lord and believe in God. No, sir, this is not me! There are certain similarities between a spiritual lifestyle and a religious lifestyle, but there are also certain differences. When we are living a spiritual lifestyle, we are free to explore the many facets of life, seeing the oneness in it all. When it comes to living a religious lifestyle in which we are a member of a religious organization, we are usually subjected to much limitations because there is only much encouragement to only follow the dictates of our clergymen and our Holy Scriptures with false claims being made such as our Holy Scriptures are the only true Holy Scriptures. What it boils down to is that there seems to be much control and manipulation in many of the religions of the world, and much narrow-mindedness. There are many religious people in the world whom think and believe that their religion is the only true religion, that their God is the only true God, that their Holy Scriptures is the only true Holy Scriptures, and so on. I also come to believe that many religious people are very selfish because they only care about what they believe in, not caring about what others believe in unless it conforms with what they believe in. Many religious people also want you to be like them. They want you to be a member of their religion. Some religious people even try to force you to conform.

Another thing that is worth mentioning now is that there is much division in the world partially because of religion. You don't have these and other problems if you were to live a spiritual lifestyle, but beware because I am certain that there are certain individuals whom claim to be spiritualists, but in reality they are charlatans whom has as their main intention to gain financially. Not only are there 'wolves in sheeps clothing' in religions, but also in spirituality, too.

As I had already mentioned to you that a spiritual lifestyle is far more superior to a materialistic lifestyle. Life upon this earth would be so much better for all of us humans if we were all to become spiritual. With all of the religions and religious people in the world, you would think that this world would be a much better place to live in. I come to believe that it is through a spiritual lifestyle, not a materialistic lifestyle or a religious lifestyle even, that the world can become a much better place for all of us humans to live in.

I feel that it is of the utmost importance that each and everyone of us humans whom are capable of practicing the techniques that are in this book should practice them so that they should develop themselves spiritually and have a much better life in the process. What do you think about all of this? Are you in a loss for words right now? Well, before I forget to mention this to you, but if you are materialistic and/or religious, please forgive me if I had offended you with any of the statements that I had made in this topic.

The Art Of Self-Discovery

'MANY OF US humans are like actors on a stage whom are playing a role that was written by others because they probably had never taken the time to discover and became their true natural selves.'

Richard R. Franza

Discovering our true natural selves is an art for sure. Just like an artist whom paints wonderful works of art, but had spent many hours in preparation, anyone whom would like to discover their true natural self will probably spend many hours in preparation for this.

The sad fact is that many of us humans are conditioned to be a certain way. This conditioning had began shortly after we had entered into this world. I know very well that much of this conditioning had served us well in the earlier stages of our lives, but you must ask yourself something right now, how is this conditioning serving us now as adults?

Take a little child. Usually they are not conditioned yet to a point in which they had lost their sense of curiosity. I come to believe that many little children have a certain amount of psychic capabilities because they are not nearly as much conditioned to be a certain way as many of us adults are. This is why I believe that Jesus Christ had advised us to be as little children if we want to enter into the Kingdom of Heaven. We need to be pure and innocent as a little child, free from being conditioned to be a certain way, if we want to enter into the Kingdom of Heaven. Talking about entering into the Kingdom of Heaven, Jesus Christ had advised us to seek the Kingdom of Heaven within above all else. The only problem is that He had not instructed us about how to do it. I come to believe that if we practice the first two techniques that are in this book, we will be in essence seeking the Kingdom of Heaven within above all else. Hey, I might be onto something extremely important right now.

Anyway, if we want to have a wonderful life-changing experience, we should discover our true natural selves first so that we can have an excellant opportunity to become our true natural selves.

On a personal note, I had discovered my true natural self and I am my true natural self on certain occasions. It seems to be much easier to discover our true natural selves than to become our true natural selves because we had been conditioned to be a certain way for probably our entire lives, and now all of a sudden we want to break free of this conditioning. Breaking free of our old conditioned self may not be an easy thing to do.

I believe that it is extremely important for us humans to discover and become our true natural selves so that we can live natural lives upon this earth. One of the main reasons why there are so many problems in the world is the fact that many of us humans are conditioned to be a certain way and we are acting in accordance with this conditioning. As extremely important it is to discover and become our true natural selves, it truly is sad and ironic that we are basically not being encouraged to do these things. Discovering and becoming our true natural selves should be a priority for us in life, but it isn't. This doesn't make any sense to me at all.

If you want to have a wonderful life-changing experience in which you should develop yourself spiritually and have a much better life, it would be to your best interest to practice the techniques that are in this book so that eventually one day you should discover and become your true natural self. Practice the techniques that are in this book, practice the techniques that are in this book, practice the techniques that are in this book!!! This is my battlecry to you.

Developing Into A Spiritual Master

WHEN I HAD discovered and began to practice the first technique that is in this book about seven years ago, all that I had wanted to do was to find a way to quit smoking crack cocaine and have much more happiness in my life. It had never dawned on me at the time that I was on the road towards becoming a spiritual master. It was a big surprise to me to find out this.

At this moment in time you may be wondering to yourself about what makes me so certain that I am developing into a spiritual master. After all, I am currently a nobody whom is from Brooklyn, New York. Well, the reason why I am certain that I am on the road towards becoming a spiritual master is that all that I need to do is to reflect back in time when I first started to practice the first technique that is in this book and see how much I had developed myself spiritually since then, and then it is easy for me to project into the future and see that I should develop myself even further spiritually to a point in which I should become a spiritual master one day.

What is a spiritual master in the first place? I will now attempt to describe to you what I consider a spiritual master to be. I consider someone to be a spiritual master when they had discovered and became their true natural self, they are in their own heavenly world quite often, not being affected by the external world (This is what I call being self-empowered), they are enlightened, they see the oneness of it all, and so on. By no means do I qualify as a spiritual master at this moment in time, but I am most definetly getting closer to becoming one.

You want to know something, I have been developing myself spiritually over the last seven years without the need of relying upon any spiritual guide to guide me. I had basically developed myself spiritually over the last seven years all on my own. Sure, I had made alot of mistakes along the way, but at least I had learned from these mistakes. I had discovered and I have been practicing the techniques that are in this book all on my own. If I could practice the techniques that are in this book all on my own, so can anyone else. I am no exception to the rule.

If you want to join me on the road towards becoming a spiritual master, I strongly suggest to you to practice the techniques that are in this book. There are no guarantees that you will eventually one day become a spiritual master by practicing these techniques, but isn't it worth taking a chance and practice these techniques anyway?

A Philosopher In Life

A CCORDING TO MY current understanding, philosophy had began in ancient Greece in the sixth century BCE. It was during this time that ancient Greece was experiencing a Golden Age with philosophy being in the forefront of it all. The ancient Greeks at the time had just about philosophized everything. Democracy had also began in ancient Greece I believe. There were many great philosophers from ancient Greece whom had sought to understand the nature of reality, and so on.

Whatever happened to philosophy in these modern times? It seems to be that philosophy is a dying art in these modern times. We are now living in an age in which we need philosophy in order to help improve the condition of this seemingly hopeless world.

It seems to be that modern man is taking everything for granted with all of the advancements in technology and all of the conveniences that are at our disposal. Modern man is also generally lacking in questioning things. We have this nasty habit of believing everything that the so-called experts have to say without questioning them. You see this happening especially with many religious people.

Another key ingredient that is philosophical in nature is the need for us humans to bring meaning to life. It seems to be that many of us humans these days are focusing so much of their attention on rather meaningless things such as their favorite sporting team wins a game or not. It never ceases to amaze me that there are many of us humans so engrossed in their favorite sporting team to a point that some of them would probably die for their favorite sporting team, and at the same time they couldn't care less about the fact that the human race is slowly becoming extinct. How on earth are us humans ever going to make this world a much better place to live in if all that we care about is if our favorite sporting team wins a game or not?

We need more philosophers in the world for sure in order to improve the condition of the world. Besides this, we need humans in the world whom are willing to take swift actions in order to try to remedy many of the problems that inflicts the human race.

On a personal note, I had became very interested in philosophy as I am developing myself spiritually. It seems to be that I had come to realize the value of being a philosopher in life if we want to have a wonderful life-changing experience. I had developed an interest in philosophy over the course of the last seven years after I had began to practice the first technique that is in this book. Us humans need to become philosophers in life so that we can also try to understand the human condition and the nature of reality.

The Glorious Golden Age Of America

YOU ARE PROBABLY wondering to yourself right now about me including this topic in a book that is about preparing ourselves for a wonderful life-changing experience. I can't blame you for this. The main reason why I had included this topic in this book is that it would be much easier to have a wonderful life-changing experience if we were to live in a wonderful nation. You are probably also wondering to yourself about me targetting America. The reason why I am targetting America is that I am an American and I would love to see firsthand my nation experiencing a glorious Golden Age.

Before I define what I mean by a glorious Golden Age, let me define what a Golden Age is. According to the dictionaries, a nation is experiencing a Golden Age when the members of that nation are experiencing a great deal of peace, prosperity, happiness, and achievements. I'm not stopping at just a Golden Age that America is experiencing, I am going one step further and would like to write about a glorious Golden Age that America would be experiencing.

If America was to ever experience a glorious Golden Age, each of us Americans would be experiencing such a magnificent life in America. All of the requirements for a nation experiencing a Golden Age would be met and so much more. If America is experiencing a glorious Golden Age, us Americans would have discovered and became our true natural selves, we would be freely sharing with each other, we would be caring about each other and our nation itself, we would be united and cooperative towards each other, and so on. If America is experiencing a glorious Golden Age, there would no longer be homeless Americans, there would no longer be racist Americans, there would no longer be wealthy Americans whom are hoarding massive amounts of wealth, there would no longer be poor Americans, there would be far less crime in America, and so on. Wouldn't these things be wonderful for sure!

There are certain reasons for the prevention of America experiencing a glorious Golden Age such as many of us Americans lack in care and concern for other fellow Americans and America itself, many Americans feel hopeless and powerless, many Americans are conditioned to be a certain way, us Americans are extremely divided and noncooperative towards each other, the leaders of

America seemingly have no interest in America experiencing a glorious Golden Age, and so on.

The first requirement that needs to be met in order for America to experience a glorious Golden Age is that each of us Americans discovers and becomes our true natural selves so that we can become true genuine human beings and benefit in many other ways. After each of us Americans discovers and becomes our true natural selves, then we must unite like a mighty team in order to resolve all of the major problems that currently plagues America, and there are many major problems that currently plagues America.

I find it hard to comprehend why us Americans are settling for what America has become. Seemingly, America is slowly deteriorating and it seems to be that all that many of us Americans cares about is money, great sex, having fun, partying, entertaining themselves, their favorite sporting team winning a game or not, and so on. Many of us Americans should be ashamed of themselves. Why aren't us Americans trying to bring out the best in ourselves so that we can bring out the best in America? So much has gone wrong in America over the last several decades, and if we continue to allow America to further deteriorate, I wouldn't be surprised that America will become a third-world nation one day. Wake up, my fellow Americans, wake up!

If you are an American and you would like to do your part in helping to bring a glorious Golden Age to America, you can start by practicing the techniques that are in this book so that eventually one day you should discover and become your true natural self.

The Tragic Fate That Awaits Mankind

Y OU ARE PROBABLY wondering to yourself right now about the title of this topic. I can't blame you for this. What I mean by the title of this topic is that mankind has a tragic fate if we keep slowly destroying our natural world. The reason why I had included this topic in this book is that how can our own future generations to come have a wonderful life-changing experience if we are slowly creating a hellish world for them to live in. We need to do something quickly because time is running out for us humans.

It is no big secret that we are slowly destroying our natural world in different ways. Us humans should be ashamed of ourselves because of the manner in which we are abusing our natural world. It seems to be that we are slowly destroying our natural world because of profitting from it at our own convenience. We are definetly taking our natural world for granted. I come to believe that two of the main reasons why we are abusing our natural world is that many of us humans had removed themselves from nature in order to live in concrete jungles and we are taking our natural world for granted. Us humans are going to pay dearly for the poor treatment of our natural world. Mankind is doomed unless we drastically change our ways.

One of the major reasons why our natural world is slowly being destroyed is that this earth is becoming overpopulated with human beings. Some drastic measures must be taken by the leaders of the world in order to help regulate and control the probable future overpopulation problem. It is because of this probable future overpopulation problem that our natural world will be abused even further, that wars will be fought, and the precious resources of this earth will be further slowly depleted at such an alarming rate.

Talking about the earth's precious resources, we are consuming earth's precious resources such as oil and coal at such an alarming rate. This doesn't make much sense to me. Us humans must act much more responsibly about this and further develop alternative methods such as solar panels that are cost effective so that we can make the most use out of the freely given, environment friendly energy that we receive from the sun. When are us humans going to wake up and truly do something towards further protecting and preserving our natural world, and conserve prescious resources? We are beyond comprehension...

'Mankind has an invetible tragic fate ahead in which they will become extinct if they continue to haphazourdly wreak havoc on our natural world and consume precious resources at such an alarming rate.'

Richard R. Franza

Entertaining Positive Thoughts

WHEN WAS THE last time that you were in the presence of a very positive person? The big secret of being a very positive person is to entertain in your mind as much positive thoughts that you can possibly entertain.

We paint our worlds generally according to the thoughts that we constantly entertain in our minds. Constantly entertain positive thoughts in your mind and your world should generally be positive. On the other hand, constantly entertain negative thoughts in your mind and your world should generally be negative.

If you want to be a success in life, try to entertain only positive thoughts, especially if you want to have a wonderful life-changing experience. I know that this may not be an easy thing to do, especially if you live in a very negative environment. Just try to do the best that you can do.

On a personal note, I am taking notice to the fact that I am becoming more positive as I continue to practice the techniques that are in this book. Being positive is becoming second-nature to me now. The only problem is that at times I am so positive, full of joy, that I get carried away. This could drive others to want to avoid you, I know this for a fact because it had happened to me on certain occasions.

Always remember that there are just certain things that we can control in life, and one of these things that we can control in life is the type of thoughts that we entertain in our minds. Therefore, know that you have the power and control over the type of thoughts that you constantly entertain in your mind.

A Strong Belief System

I T IS ALMOST three-thirty in the afternoon on a mild December day. I had just got done with some food shopping and I am preparing chicken thighs with pasta and spinach, and of course creamy vodka sauce. I have some time to write now while the chicken thighs are being prepared. I like to do two or three things at one time. Well, at least I have a very good meal to look forward to later. I love to eat like many other humans love to do. You can definetly tell that I love to eat because I weigh almost three hundred pounds. Call me 'The Happy Buddha' if you like.

Anyway, there are many humans in the world whom have a strong belief system. Many of these humans have a strong belief in God. As for me personally, I don't have a strong belief in God because I don't know if He exists or not. I am an agnostic. Admittedly, it seems to be that it is a great idea to have a strong belief in God because I clearly see that this is working wonders for many of us humans. As someone had suggested in the past that it doesn't matter if God exists or not, believe in Him anyway and see for yourself all of the wonders you will experience. This was not the exact way that he had stated it, but I think that you get the point.

I come to believe that it truly doesn't matter what we believe in. What truly matters is how deep is our conviction in what we believe in. As for me personally, I try to have a strong belief in myself. It's not easy for me to do this because I was suffering from having a low self-esteem for much of my life. It is very difficult to have a strong belief in yourself when you have a low self-esteem. At least I don't have as low of a low self-esteem these days as I did in the past.

I feel that it is of good use to have a strong belief system if we would like to have a wonderful life-changing experience. I don't think that it is essential to have a strong belief system if we want to have a wonderful life-changing experience, but it certainly doesn't hurt to have one. Strongly believe in anything that you want to, just try to have a deep conviction in what you believe in.

I think that I had been too serious with writing this book thus far. I think that it's time for a little humor. God had granted one wish to this man, anything that this man had wished for. God had said to this man: 'My son, I grant you one wish, wish for anything and you will receive it.' After thinking about it for a while, the man said to God:

'My Heavenly Father, I believe in You, I wish to receive one hundred million dollars.' God then told the man that one hundred million dollars is too much to ask for, to wish for something much less and He will grant it to him. The man then told God: 'My Heavenly Father, I wish to receive a wonderful woman to love and cherish, whom loves and cherishes me, a woman whom I can truly understand.' After hearing this from this man, God was perplexed and didn't know how to answer the man for a few moments. After thinking about it for a while, God had told the man: 'My son, how would you like to receive the one hundred million dollars, in fifties or hundreds?'

Maintaining Good Health

OH WHAT A blessing it is to have good health. We all do know this, right? Right? Right? Wrong! It seems to be that many of us humans whom have good health are taking it for granted. It's usually when something goes wrong with our health, then we realize that it's a blessing to have good health.

Why is it important to have good health? It is important to have good health, especially if we want to have a wonderful life-changing experience. I know very well that it may be very difficult to have good health for many of us Americans, including me. I currently have so many health problems that it ain't funny. I now regret it at times that when I was much younger I had abused my body at times. It had never dawned on me that I would have to pay for this when I got older. But you want to know something, there is this thing called hope. I believe that I can improve my current physical condition. Hey, it truly is paying off for me to watch Joel Osteen on Sunday morning on TV. Joel Osteen is an inspiration to me as he is one of my favorite personalities. I try to watch Joel Osteen on TV every Sunday morning at ten o'clock.

Anyway, if you want to have a wonderful life-changing experience by practicing the techniques that are in this book, it would be to your best interest to maintain good health if you can because the better you feel, the easier it is to practice the techniques that are in this book.

Working On Yourself

TALKING ABOUT THE importance of maintaining good health, the way to do it is by working on yourself on a daily basis. There are other things that you can do in order to maintain good health such as eat the right food, keep a positive attitude, have a good sense of humor because laughter is the best medicine, and so on. I feel that it is very important to put aside some time on a daily basis to work on ourselves.

What do I mean by working on yourself on a daily basis in the first place? Well, what I mean by this is that you perform certain exercises that will serve to strengthen yourself spiritually, physically, mentally, and emotionally. There are certain things that you can do to work on yourself such as physical exercises which includes a form of matial arts such as Tai-chi, self-message work, deep breathing visualization healing technique, but I feel that the most important thing that you can do when it comes to working on yourself is to practice the techniques that are in this book.

Speaking just for me, I usually work on myself at least five days a week, between three to five hours a day. I enjoy working on myself and I am dedicated to working on myself, but don't get me wrong, there are times in which I need to motivate myself to work on myself. To be totally honest with you, I am somewhat of a lazy person. I don't like being lazy because in a way I consider doing certain things as being a burdeon. I am trying to do something about my laziness, but at least I am ambitious enough to do things that I need to do such as writing this book with the hope that I can be of service to others such as yourself. I truly hope that through this book I will encourage others such as yourself to practice the techniques that are in this book so that they have a chance to have a wonderful life-changing experience as what had happened to me, and it seems to be that my life is only getting better and better by continuing to practice the techniques that are in this book. Practice the techniques that are in this book, practice the techniques that are in this book, practice the techniques that are in this book!!! You deserve to have the best life that you can possibly have. You deserve to have a wonderful life-changing experience, but you need to work at it because a wonderful life-changing experience usually doesn't come to you freely on a silver platter. Work on yourself on a daily basis, take my advice right now won't you. It is to your advantage to work on yourself on a daily basis. Try to put aside some time on a daily basis to work on yourself.

The Initial Struggle

'THERE IS A price to pay for having anything good come to your life. This price that you should pay for practicing the techniques that are in this book so that you can have an excellant opportunity to have a wonderful life-changing experience is that you should experience an initial struggle with yourself.'

Richard R. Franza

Yes, there is most definetly a price that you should pay if you were to practice the techniques that are in this book, you should experience an initial struggle with yourself. There is no other way around it. Remember, you were probably conditioned to be a certain way for just about your entire life, and now you want to break free of this conditioning. Your old conditioned self doesn't give up very easily. You will probably have to battle with yourself for quite some time after you begin to practice the techniques that are in this book.

Speaking just for me, I had to deal with an initial struggle when I had began to practice the first technique that is in this book. I wanted to give up on practicing these techniques many times, but thank God that I didn't. I had to deal with all of those rough moments that I was confronted with.

I must give you this fair warning, if you intend to practice the techniques that are in this book, expect to experience an initial struggle with yourself. Don't worry if this happens to you because this initial struggle should lessen as time progresses. Prepare yourself for a battle between your true natural self and your conditioned self if you were to begin to practice the techniques that are in this book.

The Suggested Techniques

BEFORE I GO into writing about this topic, I would like to share with you something that troubles me very much so. You see, there is such an extremely unfair distribution of wealth in the world that is creating a great deal of problems for much of the human race. According to my current understanding, about only one percent of the world's population is in possession of most of the wealth in the world. This is totally absurd! It is because of this that there are so many humans in the world whom are being deprived of basic necessities, many of these humans are even dying from starvation. How can we allow the chosen fortunate one's to hoarde such a massive amount of wealth in which is depriving so many other humans of a chance of living a descent life?

I believe that there is enough wealth in the world for every human being to live a comfortable life. In order for this to happen, there must be a much fairer distribution of wealth. Why on earth are the leaders of the world not trying to do anything towards preventing this extremely unfair distribution of wealth? And, why are we also allowing this extremely unfair distribution of wealth to happen right before our eyes?

Anyway, now is the time to unveil to you the actual techniques that I am currently practicing, but before I do this, I would like to raise certain issues with you again about these techniques.

For starters, it may seem to be very overwhelming to practice the fifteen techniques. It is not overwhelming to do this. I feel that it is essential to practice the first two techniques and then you can choose to practice any which one's of the other thirteen techniques that you wish to practice. If you are uncomfortable with practicing anyone of the other thirteen techniques, don't practice it.

The next issue that I wish to raise with you is that you must have patience and perseverance, especially in the beginning, if you are just beginning to practice the techniques that are in this book because it may take quite some time to get accustomed to practicing them and for them to become effective.

The next issue that I wish to raise with you is that you are the boss. You can practice the techniques that are in this book any which way you wish to. I only will suggest to you how I currently practice the techniques.

And finally, the last issue that I wish to raise with you is that I am not in the conversion business. Come as you are regardless of what your background is. By practicing the techniques that are in this book, this should help to serve to enhance your life's experiences.

There you have it! I will now unveil to you the actual techniques, but before I do this, I strongly suggest to you to at least consider to practice them because it will be to your own good to practice them. I want you to have the best life that you can possibly have. I am only sharing with you a proven way on how your life should eventually become a wonderful life to live if you were to practice the techniques that are in this book. This is what had happened to me, and I know that this could also happen to you, too. Please refer to the following sub-topics that consists of the actual techniques that I am currently practicing with the hope that you will also practice them:

I) A Constant Meditative State

This technique is the first technique that I had discovered and began to practice about seven years ago. I consider this technique as the most important technique to practice because it is about controlling our minds, and if we want to do anything in life with effectiveness, it would be to our best interest to have control of our minds first.

You may be wondering to yourself right now that how can it be possible for anyone to be in a constant meditative state. Well, I can't blame you for this. The manner in which we can be in a constant meditative state is that we can be in a very mild constant meditative state while we are in public, and be in a deeper constant meditative state when we are in places such as in the privacy of our own homes.

If you are interested in practicing this technique, all that you need to do is to try to relax your mind, try to be at total peace with yourself, and try to be fully absorbed in the present moment. Try to either silence your mind completely or only think about something that is necessary at the moment. Try to rid your mind of all unnecessary thoughts. Try to make life a meditation.

II) Focusing on Your Inner Self

This technique is the second technique that I had discovered and began to practice about seven years ago. I consider this technique as the second most important technique to practice because it is about detaching ourselves from the outer world by turning within ourselves in which we should be developing our intuition and rely upon the master within ourselves for guidance. By focusing on our inner selves we are also turning within ourselves where true joy and true happiness can be found.

If you are interested in practicing this technique, all that you need to do is to slightly withdraw your senses from the outer world and focus as much of your attention on your inner self as you possibly can.

As a reminder, if you intend to practice the two techniques that I had just shared with you in this book, I suggest to you to only practice the first technique first until you get reasonably comfortable with practicing it, and then you can also practice the second technique.

III) Reciting Positive Affirmations

The human brain is similar to a computer system in the sense that it can be 'programmed' to think in a certain way. What better way is there to 'program' our brains than to repeat a certain statement over and over again?

A positive affirmation is a statement that is of a positive nature. If you intend to recite positive affirmations, all that you need to do is to comfortably sit in a place of privacy while staring out into space directly in front of you. Take a deep breath and then after exhaling, slowly audibly recite a positive affirmation at least ten times. Try to use your imagination and put your feelings into it for much better results. You can audibly recite as many positive affirmations that you wish to. As an example of what kind of positive affirmations that you can audibly recite is: 'I love myself.' Try to audibly recite positive affirmations once daily. Before I forget to mention to you that if you are reciting positive affirmations, pause for at least one minute in between one positive affirmation to the next positive affirmation.

IV) Using Your Imagination

The imagination that us humans possess is a powerful tool to possess if we were to properly use it. We could bring into reality simple and realistic things with the proper use of our imagination. As an example, at times I imagine my face to have a smile upon it. Sure enough, my face develops a genuine smile and I feel happier.

If you intend to practice this technique, all that you need to do is to fully focus on what you are imagining for a certain period of time. Naturally, you can use your imagination anytime that you wish to.

V) Performing A Ritual

A ritual is a great way to train us humans to be a certain way when we are performing it. It is very easy to construct a ritual. All that you need to do is to derive certain statements that are of a positive nature and use corresponding gestures while audibly reciting these statements. Try to use your imagination and put your feelings into it if you are performing a ritual for much better results.

If you intend to practice this technique, stand in a place of privacy, stare out into space directly in front of you, take a deep breath, then after exhaling, slowly audibly recite a statement that is of a positive nature while using a corresponding gesture, then pause for about fifteen seconds, then repeat the process by using another statement and corresponding gesture. You can make your ritual as long as you want to make it.

As an example, during one part of my ritual I audibly recite: 'I love myself' while I am hugging myself. I suggest to you to perform a ritual once daily.

At this moment in time I would like to backtrack to when I had written about the issues that I wish to raise with you again in this topic about practicing these techniques that are in this book. I had forgotten to mention to you again that if you were to practice the techniques that are in this book, there are no guarantees that you will eventually have a wonderful life-changing experience in which you should develop yourself spiritually and have a much better life, and I am not responsible for your outcome if you were to practice the techniques that are in this book. I do believe that if you were to properly practice the techniques that are in this book, eventually one day you should have a wonderful life-changing experience.

VI) Performing A Self-Hypnosis

A great way to access our subconscious minds is through performing a self-hypnosis. There are many ways to perform a self-hypnosis. The way that I currently perform my self-hypnosis is that I stare at a beautiful woman for a while whom is walking on by. Hey, if a beautiful woman can't mesmerize us men, something is seriously wrong. Just joking with you right now even though there is some truth in this joke.

Anyway, the way that I currently perform a self-hypnosis is that I sit in a comfortable position in a place of privacy, staring out into space directly in front of me, I take five deep breaths, after the exhalation of the fifth deep breath I audibly recite: 'I am in my own heavenly world,' then I pause for about fifteen seconds, then I close my eyes and slowly recite the same statement internally four times, then I pause for about fifteen seconds, then I open my eyes and take a deep breath, after exhaling I audibly recite the same statement, then I pause for about fifteen seconds, and then I am finished. If I properly perform my self-hypnosis, I usually go into a trancelike state and into my own heavenly world from one extent to another extent. I also try to use my imagination and put my feelings into it when I am performing my self-hypnosis.

If you intend to practice this technique, you can try to do it the way that I do it or you can come up with your own way of doing it. Try to perform a self-hypnosis once daily.

VII) Performing A Self-Analysis

Many of us humans are so accustomed to having others analize us. I don't think that there is anything wrong with this, but we can also analize ourselves so that we should be able to understand ourselves better. It is not that difficult to perform a self-analysis, but if you were to perform a self-analysis, try to be open-minded and honest with yourself, try to find out the reasons why you think and behave a certain way. You can perform a self-analysis anytime that you wish to perform it.

VIII) Opening Your Heart To Love

If you were to open your heart to love, you should be experiencing unconditional love for everyone and everything. It is easy to open your heart to love. All that you need to do is to focus on your heart, trying to feel a warm sensation in it. You can open your heart to love anytime that you wish to do it.

IX) Reciting A Daily Affirmation

What better way is there to start your day than reciting a daily affirmation? All that a daily affirmation is is a group of sentences that should be of a positive nature. It is easy to construct a daily affirmation. All that you need to do is derive sentences that are of a positive nature, making your daily affirmation as long as you want to make it. As an example, you can start your daily affirmation with: 'I am thankful to have another wonderful day of life. It is going to be a wonderful day for me.'

If you intend to practice this technique, all that you need to do is to comfortably sit in a place of privacy, take a deep breath and then after exhaling, slowly audibly recite your daily affirmation. Try to use your imagination and put your feelings into it while you are audibly reciting your daily affirmation. It's that simple. Try to recite a daily affirmation once daily in the morning preferrably.

X) Writing And Reciting A Statement

What better way is there to leave an impression on our minds than to repeatedly write a statement and then audibly reciting them? All that you need to do in order to practice this technique is to comfortably sit in a place of privacy, take a deep breath and then after exhaling, write a statement that is of a positive nature ten times, then after doing this, slowly audibly recite this statement starting from the first one to the last one. Try to use your imagination and put your feelings into it for much better results. As an example, you can use: 'I am very happy' as the statement to write and recite. Try to write and recite a statement once daily.

XI) Staring In The Mirror

Another way to leave an impression on your mind is to stare in the mirror for about one minute, try to put a gentle smile upon your face as you gaze into your eyes, doing this in a place of privacy, take a deep breath and then after exhaling, slowly audibly recite statements that are of a positive nature such as: 'I feel real good about myself.' Try to stare in the mirror once daily.

XII) Self-Talk

By practicing this technique, you can monitor what you tell yourself. All that you need to do if you want to practice this technique is either verbally or internally tell yourself things that should be of a positive nature such as: 'I am very happy today.' Naturally, you can practice this technique anytime that you wish to practice it.

XIII) Opening Your Chakras

Before I write about this sub-topic, I must mention something to you first. If you were to practice anyone of the techniques that are in this book, try to fully focus on what you are doing. By fully focusing and concentrating on what you are doing in the present moment should greatly help you to receive much better results with what you are doing at the moment.

According to my current understanding, the chakras are energy centers that links our physical bodies to the etheric region. The human body has seven chakras. When we open our chakras and energy is freely flowing through them, we should experience a wonderful sensation in our bodies. The two chakras that I love to open and feel energy flowing through them are the crown chakra which is located above the top of our heads, and the heart chakra which is located slightly to the right of our hearts, in the solar plexis area.

If you are interested in practicing this technique, I suggest to you to employ the use of your imagination and try to imagine energy flowing in the area where a chakra is located. I also suggest to you to do some research about the chakras of the human body. You can try to open your chakras anytime that you wish to try to open them.

XIV) Focusing On The Universal Energy Field

Many of us humans limit themselves because they are only focusing their attention on the boundaries of this physical world. These humans are depriving themselves of experiencing the oneness of it all by not 'tuning into' the universal energy field. The universal energy field is the energy that animates all physical objects that is in this physical universe. It is just one unimaginable energy field.

If you want to experience such wonderful sensations, try to focus your attention on the universal energy field by either imagining it and\or by feeling it. You should empty your vessel of all thoughts and emotions first. You can practice this technique anytime that you wish to practice it.

XV) Gazing Out Into Space Above

Again, many of us humans limit themselves because they are only focusing their attention on the boundaries of this physical world. These humans are depriving themselves of such wonderful sensations by ignoring this vast universe and our place in it. There are so many extraordinary things occurring out there in space.

It was not too long ago that I had started to spend some time gazing out into space above. I like to do this especially when I am listening to good music from the past when I am outdoors. Quite often when I gaze out into space above I am so elated to a point in which I feel as if I had taken a strong drug.

If you want to practice this technique, I suggest to you to gaze out into space above, trying to imagine what is happening out there while listening to music that you love to listen to and is uplifting. You can practice this technique anytime that you wish to practice it.

There you have it! I had just shared with you fifteen invaluable techniques that if properly practiced, you should eventually one day have a wonderful life-changing experience in which you should develop yourself spiritually and have a much better life. Practice these techniques! Practice these techniques! Practice these techniques!!!

The Benefits

THERE ARE MANY benefits that I am receiving from practicing the techniques that are in this book. Please refer to the following list of much of these many benefits:

1) I had discovered my true natural self and I am my true natural self on certain occasions.

2) I have much more happiness in my life now than I had ever had before in my life.

3) I am becoming self-empowered.

4) I am becoming enlightened.

5) I am becoming very moral.

6) I am developing a very keen sense of awareness.

7) I am becoming much more creative.

8) I am becoming much more caring.

9) I am living in the present moment much more now than ever before in my life.

10) I am becoming a refined human being.

11) I am becoming less fearful about death.

12) I am now much more interested in gaining knowledge than I had ever been before in my life.

13) I am now less stressful than I had ever been for much of my life.

14) I had became desireless towards abusing alcohol and illegal drugs.

15) My mental illness had became greatly alleviated.

16) I am now experiencing more:

    I)   Peace,

    II) Tranquility,

    III) Calmness,

    IV) Harmony,

    V) Serenity,

    VI) And joy.

17) I now go into my own heavenly world on certain occasions.

Etc.

The Pitfalls

IT IS ONLY fair that I share with you much of the pitfalls that I am experiencing from practicing the techniques that are in this book. The good news is that these pitfalls are lessening as time progresses. Please refer to the following list of much of these pitfalls:

1) I had developed a strong inner urge to reach out and help others. I am experiencing a good deal of disappointment from doing this because it seems to be that many humans are in dire need of being helped, but they are reluctant to accept help from others such as myself for one reason or another.

2) I am somewhat obsessed with practicing the techniques that are in this book.

3) I am not mindful at times.

4) I am experiencing more loneliness now because when you journey on the road towards developing yourself spiritually, it seems to be that you have to go it all alone.

5) I am feeling down at times because after an uplifting experience happens and the elation of it wears off, I want to go back to experiencing this elation again and I might not be able to do it.

6) I feel down at times because now I am able to see the reality of physical life on earth much clearer than ever before. I can clearly see that many of us humans of this world are not approaching life properly. The reality of it all is that us humans are creating a great deal of problems for ourselves, and we had also created a very dangerous world to live in. By knowing these things, how can anyone not feel a little depressed at times?

7) I had became a little lazier now because life had slowed down for me. It seems to be that I have to motivate myself more now in order to do things.

Etc.

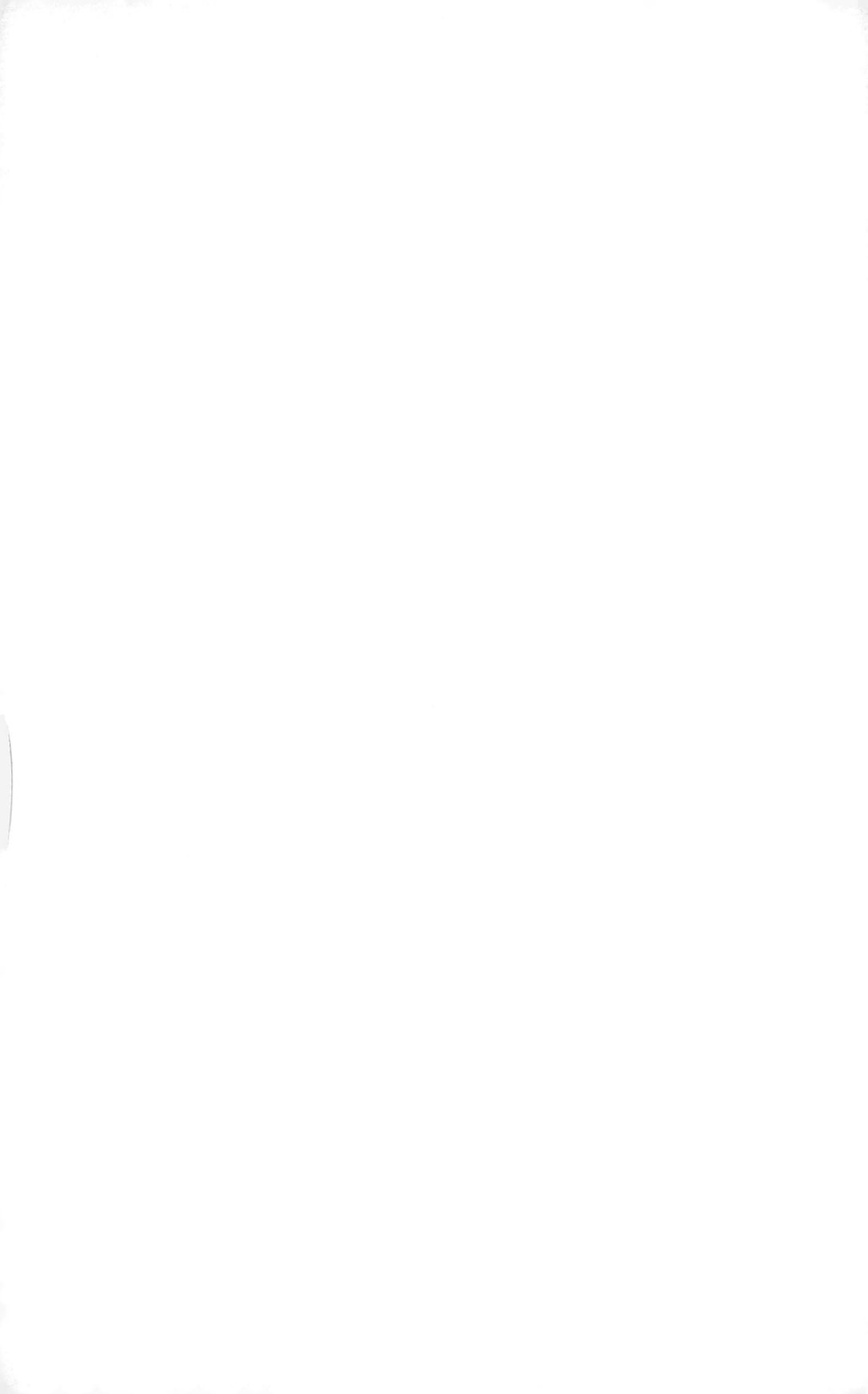

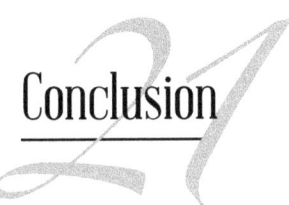

Conclusion

I HAD JUST FINISHED reading the entire manuscript of this book upto this point. I feel that I had done a good job thus far with writing this book. I don't know if you were able to detect that after reading this entire book upto this point, I had taken much more time in writing it in the beginning stages, and then in the latter stages of this book I had rushed a little in writing it. That's okay I guess. What do you think about this book thus far? Was I able to motivate you to at least consider to practice the techniques that are in this book? As I had already mentioned to you in the introduction that my main goal is to motivate you to practice the techniques that are in this book. Now tell me, did I do a good job to get you to at least consider to practice these techniques?

As you can clearly see that I had kept my word when I had mentioned to you in this book that there is an immense amount of vital information in it, but the fun is not over yet. There is more to come. Read on and see that there is more vital information to come. I hope that you had not only enjoyed reading this book upto this point, but also may the information in it serves you well.

A Special Bonus

PREPARE YOURSELF FOR a truly wonderful life-changing experience

I WILL NOW SHARE with you one hundred invaluable suggestions that should greatly help you towards having a truly wonderful life-changing experience. Please refer to the following list of one hundred invaluable suggestions:

1) Discover and become your true natural self by practicing the techniques that are in this book.

2) Be a spiritualist in life. Leave the materialistic lifestyle behind if you are materialistic.

3) Work on yourself on a daily basis in order to strengthen yourself spiritually, physically, mentally, and emotionally.

4) Care about others, your nation, and our natural world.

5) Entertain only positive thoughts in your mind.

6) Associate yourself with others whom are uplifting.

7) Have at least one hobby that you love to do.

8) Stand for a worthy cause in life.

9) Identify yourself with your spirit. Fully realize that you are not your physical body.

10) Wish others all the best in life instead of hating others, thinking that you are better than others, holding grudges towards others, being jealous of others, and judging others harshly.

11) If you are employable, have a job that you love to do.

12) Be a member of a wonderful organization such as The Rosicrucian Order. I am a proud member of The Rosicrucian Order.

13) Love yourself above all other loves.

14) Love life in it's entirety.

15) Don't care about what others think about you. Only care about what you think about yourself.

16) Be a philosopher in life.

17) Be grateful for everything in life.

18) Be humble by knowing the truth that us humans are just tiny microrganisms whom exist on a tiny pebble called 'earth' that is lost out in this vast universe.

19) Be curious as a little child.

20) Expose yourself to only positive stimuli if you can.

21) Don't abuse your body with any harmful substances, and if you do, do it in moderation.

22) Maintain good health if you can.

23) Learn from the true masters in life.

24) Be open-minded because you can learn something from just about everyone.

25) Have a strong belief system. It truly doesn't matter what you believe in just as long as you strongly believe in it.

26) Have the right partner for you in life. Don't settle for anything less.

27) Only conduct activities that are of a moral nature.

28) Listen to your master within above all else. Let your intuition be your guide.

29) Avoid all types of confrontations.

30) Don't try to convince anyone or try to prove a point to them.

31) Step outside the box and expand your awareness.

32) Don't fear death. Know deeply that death is a natural process.

33) Always remain calm under all circumstances.

34) Be kind and considerate towards others.

35) Have a sense of humor.

36) Yearn for knowledge. Try to gain as much knowledge as you possibly can in many subjects.

37) Nurture good qualities such as honesty, integrity, respectability, and dignity.

38) Don't try to please others or try to draw attention to yourself.

39) Live a simple and meager lifestyle.

40) Don't follow the crowd.

41) Don't complain about anything, do something about it.

42) Know that we are all equal regardless of who we are and what our position in life is.

43) Live in the present moment because the present moment is the only reality.

44) Tread slowly through life.

45) Discover your natural rhythm and move to it.

46) Always remain self-centered if you can.

47) Deeply know that life is eternal.

48) Give back to life, especially if life is being good to you.

49) Deeply know that everything is energy in one form or in another form.

50) Feel the oneness of all things.

51) Be gentle with your physical body.

52) Eat only when hungry. Fast from eating for a long period of time from time to time.

53) Don't worry about anything because worrying is like a poison to our bodies.

54) Speak but few words effectively.

55) Be an observer in life.

56) Don't look at others as sex objects.

57) Be a mystery to others.

58) Don't love money or any other material thing.

59) Deeply know that physical life is but a dream.

60) Know that you are a mystery that needs to be unraveled.

61) Don't seek to control others.

62) Consider problems as blessings in disguise.

63) Know that you are creating your own reality for the most part with your thoughts.

64) Focus on meaningful things.

65) See beauty in the ugliest of things. See even more beauty in the most beautiful of things.

66) Make life purposeful.

67) Focus only on positive things.

68) Repay hatred with kindness.

69) Always be diplomatic when dealing with others.

70) Always be pleasant to others.

71) Concentrate on what you are doing.

72) Appreciate things in life.

73) Try to understand others by realizing that they are having their own personal experiences in life.

74) Always be yourself.

75) Set a goal, believing that you had already achieved it.

76) Get interested in others.

77) Visualize the kind of life that you would like to have.

78) Try to do your part in helping to make this world a much better place to live in.

79) Know that we affect each other. That is why it is important that we send out positive vibrations.

80) Think very highly of yourself, but not in an arrogant or conceited manner.

81) Properly play your role as a man if you are a man, and as a woman if you are a woman.

82) Don't allow others to discourage you from what you are doing unless you shouldn't be doing it.

83) Plan your day and try to stick to your plans.

84) Don't play games with others.

85) Face life with a gentle smile on your face.

86) Don't judge others based on their appearance.

87) Don't take things personally.

88) See the beauty in everyone.

89) Don't allow anyone to ruin the wonderful day that you should be having.

90) Try to do things wholeheartedly.

91) Always be fair in your dealings with others.

92) Do things in life that will make you feel proud of yourself.

93) Look forward to doing things. Have good expectations with these things.

94) Don't consider anyone else as an enemy.

95) Look at the beauty of the heavenly sky above from time to time.

96) Don't seek to be in competition with anyone else unless it is absolutely necessary.

97) When someone does you wrong, don't look to take revenge against them.

98) Deeply know that you never know what the next moment shall bring to you in life.

99) Feel good about yourself.

100) Realize that it's a priveledge to have a physical body and to be able to exist on this planet called 'earth.'

There you have it! I had just shared with you one hundred invaluable suggestions that can lead you towards having a truly wonderful life-changing experience. Now do as you please with these one hundred invaluable suggestions.

Philosophical Quotes of the Day

1) 'What came first, God or humans?'

2) 'If we only focus on the half-full portion of a glass and ignore the half-empty portion, perhaps one day the glass shall be completely empty.'

3) 'If we are going to love anything in life, instead of loving a tiny piece of paper, money, let's love the sun that gives us life.'

4) 'Many of us humans are drowning in their own ignorance.'

5) 'If God is love and He watches over us, then how could it be possible that He would even think about condemning anyone of us to eternal hellfire on judgement day?'

6) 'If we rely upon the leaders of this world to guide us, boy oh boy, are we in for rough times ahead.'

7) 'Be dead to this world if you want to truly live.'

8) 'The only thing that us humans need to be saved from is our own ignorance.'

9) 'What's the big deal about money and sex?'

10) 'You never know what the next moment shall bring to you in life.'

11) 'Count your blessings while you still have them.'

12) 'This world is full of actors upon a stage, playing a role that was written by others.'

13) 'Humans should not be fighting against each other and killing each other as the animals in the wild do.'

14) 'We only harm ourselves when we hate others.'

15) 'There are many problems to the left of me, there are many problems to the right, but I only look straight ahead and move on.'

16) 'Many of us humans are depriving themselves from having such a magnificent life.'

17) 'It's the same old game of the aristocrats versus the common people, and the usual results is that the aristocrats are winning.'

18) 'I simply 'kick-back' and watch many of us humans make fools out of themselves.'

19) 'Many of us humans are subtle economic slaves and they don't even realize it.'

20) 'Why should I waste my precious time with chasing after things of this world when the kingdom of heaven upon this earth is at hand?'

21) 'Follow the ways of this world and this will lead you to your own demise.'

22) 'Many of us humans should be ashamed of themselves because the human race is slowly heading towards extinction and all that they seem to care about is whether or not their favorite sporting team wins a game.'

23) 'If you want to become wealthy one day, become a popular televangelist.'

24) 'Why are you focusing only on the clouds around the sun and not focusing only on the sun?'

25) 'I don't complain. I do something about it.'

26) 'It seems to be that every human being thinks that they are always right. I'm still waiting to come across just one human being whom thinks that they can be wrong at times.'

27) 'What you now see will not be one day.'

28) 'There are just two things in life that are certain: death and rebirth.'

29) 'True wisdom is not in knowing, but in not knowing with curiosity to know.'

30) 'When you experience eternity in the present moment, it is then that you can surely live.'

Certain Facts About Me

I AM A PROUD American whom is of mostly Italian ancestry, I was born and raised in Brooklyn, New York, I am a non-practicing Catholic, I am a proud member of The Rosicrucian Order, I am an Operation Desert Storm veteran, I am a writer, and I am a spiritualist.

I was born and raised in Brooklyn, New York and I had lived there until I had joined the US Army when I was eighteen years old. I had an interesting upbringing in Brooklyn. At times I was on the wrong side of the law, and I had began abusing alcohol at the age of thirteen, I had began abusing illegal drugs at the age of fourteen. I had abused alcohol and illegal drugs until the age of fifty-one when I had became desireless towards abusing these things because of discovering and practicing some of the techniques that are in this book. By far the best times that I had in my youth was when disco music was at it's peak. I had such a wonderful time going to the discoteches with my friends.

At the age of eighteen I had enlisted into the US Army for four years. I had done alot of traveling during these four years and was even stationed in Germany for two years. I was not one for the Army life. After I was discharged from the US Army, I moved back to Brooklyn and received an Associates Degree in Electronic Technology. At this time I had met my ex-wife. We have two wonderful sons and five wonderful grandchildren now.

I had joined the Army National Guard in 1988. My unit was activated during Operation Desert Shield in 1990, and in 1991 we were sent to Saudi Arabia right before the beginning of Operation Desert Storm. We were in The Middle East region for five full months. I did not participate in the actual fighting during Operation Desert Storm, but I was in an area that was struck by scud missiles two or three times a week during the war. I had also went into Kuwait and Iraq shortly after the ceasefire. I had saw alot of wreakage and devastation, and some humans whom were burnt to a crisp.

I had began working at Long Island University in 1988 as a Physics Lab Technician. It was such a wonderful experience for me to work at Long Island University. The human beings whom also worked there were so wonderful to associate with, and I had loved my job there and all of my responsibilities. I had worked at Long Island University until in my fourteenth year working there I had a freaky bar accident. Unfortunately, I had to eventually leave my job at Long Island University because I had developed excruciating headaches that was driving me insane. This is when I had began my ten year abuse with crack cocaine. I was suffering so much from these headaches that I had even attempted to commit suicide by purposely getting lost out in the desert in Arizona. I had almost died there, but luckily I was found by others. Thank God these headaches had gone away.

My ten year crack cocaine addiction was the worst ten years of my life, but before going into this, I would like to mention that I was working on my second degree, a Master's Degree, in Computer Science while I was working at Long Island University, but I had to end it abruptly because of my excruciating headaches. Again, my ten year crack cocaine addiction was the worst ten years of my life. I was a slave to this substance. I had done so many grimy things when I was a crack cocaine addict. I was homeless at times, I was conducting some criminal activities, and I had even practically sold my soul to the devil during my ten year crack cocaine addiction. Besides this, I was diagnosed with certain mental disorders, and even instituted in psyche wards about fifteen times during my ten year crack cocaine addiction and shortly afterwards.

My life had gotten tremendously better these days as I am now living the kind of life that I more or less wish to live. I am a disabled veteran right now, but I try to keep myself busy. I now practice so many types of exercises, I am a writer, I should soon begin my mission to try to reach out and help my fellow Americans, and so on. I am currently living in Brooklyn, a client of a wonderful housing program, ICL. I think that I have a very bright future ahead of me if I was to take better care of my health and all goes well. We will see just what the future will bring to me.

I will close this book with the following short poem that I am sharing with you, the reader of this book:

I Wish For This To Happen To You

My good friend,

I hope that your time was well spent

During reading this book in it's entirety

If you did do this,

I want you to know that

Even though I may not know you,

I care about you

Cause

You are a brother or a sister of mine

Cause

You are also a member of our human race

And we

Are closely tied to each other

While we exist upon this earth.

My good friend,

I want you to know right now that

Much joy will be brought to my heart

If this book serves you well

And you begin to practice

The techniques that are in it,

Especially if one day

A wonderful life-changing experience

Occurs in your life;

I wish for this to happen to you.

                                        Richard R. Franza

Embrace This Lifetime

I HAD THOUGHT THAT I had closed this book with the preceeding poem, but at the last minute I had decided to include this topic in this book because I feel that it is very important for each of us humans to have a full understanding that we should embrace this lifetime.

You see, much of the human race lacks in wisdom for sure, and one of the reasons for this is that many of us humans consider this lifetime of existing in this physical realm in a humanly form as a burdeon to them without realizing that we are priveledged to be here existing upon this earth as humans. Look, I know very well that life can be very challenging at times for us humans, but challenges are a good thing because they help to make us grow. Here we are, many of us humans are trying to escape from life by doing destructive things to themselves such as abusing alcohol and/or illegal drugs. Many of us humans are chasing after things that may only bring to them temporal pleasure. Many of us humans had even bought into the idea that money brings happiness to our lives. The heck with money. I couldn't care less if I have one billion dollars in the bank or only one hundred dollars as long as I am reasonably comfortable. I know that money can't buy us happiness, and if it does buy us happiness, then it is a false sense of happiness.

There are many humans whom can't wait to end their time upon this earth because they had bought into the idea that when they do die their souls will go to heaven for eternity. If they can't wait to get to heaven when they die, why don't they just kill themselves now in order to get their lives upon this earth over with? Just joking about this. I don't like the idea that when I die my soul will be going to a heavenly paradise for eternity. This sounds very boring to me. I want to experience being in a physical form for a lifetime and then after my physical form perishes, I want to be in a heavenly paradise for a certain period of time until I get reincarnated into another physical form so that I will be able to experience life again in this physical realm. Whom on earth wants to be in a heavenly paradise for eternity anyway? Many humans want this it seems.

Us humans are very fortunate to be in a humanly form, existing upon this earth regardless how trying this lifetime is for us. We need to embrace this lifetime for sure. Instead of looking at life as being problematic, we should be thankful to have this life as it is and feel as if we are truly blessed because we are truly blessed to be in a humanly form, existing upon this earth. Embrace this lifetime if you are not doing this already. Be a very fortunate human being by knowing that you are very fortunate to be a human being whom is existing on such a magnificent planet that is in this unimaginably vast universe. Have a truly wonderful life.

<u>The End!</u>

Lightning Source UK Ltd.
Milton Keynes UK
UKHW041352090119
335177UK00001B/11/P